FIRSTMATTERPRESS
Portland, Ore.

ALSO BY ASH GOOD

sounds in my möbius mind
These things will never happen quite like that again
I watch you find the sum in your obsession with a part (chapbook)
Years grew a keloid (chapbook)

WE
ARE
NOT
READY
FOR
WHAT
WE
ARE

Copyright © 2019 by Ash Good
All rights reserved

Published in the United States
by First Matter Press
Portland, Oregon

Names, details and locations in this
work may have been altered to
protect privacy or may resemble actual
occurrences, persons or places; these
stories are woven of poetic memory
and best regarded as fanciful

Paperback ISBN 978-0-9972987-8-9

Cover and Interior Illustrations
Copyright © 2018 by Hellsea
www.hellsea-art.com

Book design & typography
by Ash Good www.ashgood.design

FIRSTMATTERPRESS.ORG

WE ARE NOT READY FOR WHAT WE ARE

ash good

FIRSTMATTERPRESS
Portland, Ore.

"My water body wanted to go her own way and so she did . . ."

—BIRCH DWYER

POEMS

- *12* he says it is hard to imagine me unkind
- *14* when she dies i wonder if your grandmother is still alive
- *16* after someone is gone how long do you keep breathing them in?
- *18* it seeps in somehow that eyes line my marrow

- *22* in these conversational interjections that i am once married
- *24* what crashes inside
- *27* we eat family-style & our progeny are theoretical
- *28* our mothers are different

34 "nowhere do i want to remain folded"
36 this pendulum of away, erase, return, fuse, recleave
38 stretching farther back than math, ever present wisdom if i let it
41 in & out of the ache of this ten-toed shape

46 i remember how to transmute what i can't forget
49 a mage shows me there is a womb big enough to hold all of me
51 afterward
52 release at the prompt of an elegy

*"the thirteen organs of our living are
the thirteen organs of our dying"*

—TAO TE CHING

HE SAYS IT IS HARD TO IMAGINE ME UNKIND

but i don't suspect it is for you
less imagining than reliving
my snap of impatience

i wish sometimes you could know me
now that i try to be kind
done over i will break up differently—

avoid fulfilling ghost prophecies
i am no longer that ferocious
girl trapped in our story

can you bring her to me?
she needs kindness
only i am not always kind

when he makes me late for my kuni's funeral
i slip into comfortable sharpness
with clipped measured tone

what fucking planet is this okay on?
the clench of my jaw for twenty-eight miles
my poor parking job

how i move the shift knob too hard & let the door slam
i know i am not always kind
it's a long walk across this cemetery

toward my small huddled family
prayers already in motion
bringing the shadow you know with me

WHEN SHE DIES I WONDER IF YOUR GRANDMOTHER IS STILL ALIVE

on the day of my great aunt's last breath i drive
thirty-seven-and-a-half miles
sit on the daveneau & tell my gran again

i don't want a cold coke
no one cries or even acknowledges why i arrive
you know my family only does death in passing stories—

the grade school acquaintance's mother who succumbs
to melanoma that keeps growing for twenty-seven years
the old man up the road ya know his wife gave up the ghost

& she was the only one who drove him everywhere
i go outside
gramp's too old to prune backyard vines

tangling through tall rhododendrons
heavy with black fruit
mama joins me with dull shears from the barn

she cuts
i pick
fill coffee can after mixing bowl

i am beating
still
younger & stronger than i ever notice

my body's anthem
the unexpected fire
where thorn wakes skin

AFTER SOMEONE IS GONE HOW LONG DO YOU KEEP BREATHING THEM IN?

i clean off her bathroom sink
trashing lotion bottles
finger-smudged with her red lipstick

the navy & gold tube too
half gone & mottled
it doesn't occur to me until evening

the finality—how maybe i
should have tucked all this away
in a container to consider later

as though a box of used toiletries in the closet
might materialize
her shaky hand again

holding
estée lauder
this dresser smells of her

perhaps i should replace the liners
add a sachet of cedar
but for now i only fix the knob

knocking around the corners of the top right drawer
i lift stacks of tanks & bras &
the whole of warm winter

fabric i won't wear for another season
into these caverns
i consider burning sage but am instead convinced

the potion of my things will permeate this wood
from the inside
some alchemy in her legacy cradling mine

IT SEEPS IN SOMEHOW THAT EYES LINE MY MARROW

the cashier's name tag says elizabeth & she smells
the flowers i buy
a hefty spray of salmon-hued gladiolus

six more stems of petals i can't place the name of
i bought the dark purple ones last week
she lifts the gladiolus toward me

the next day the blooms all opened — beautiful
i didn't used to just buy myself flowers
but then i started paying attention to what my ancestors want

you know pour them a little coffee
ask what they'd like
flowers they said

i feel your *a-yèh* & his smoldering sticks
incense lit daily to worship his origin
how his turns into the only dead body i see

we get in trouble for laughing
in that small parlor room—
some quip i don't recall

your embarrassed ma's glare
our misunderstood non sequitur to escape four
rows of mostly empty folding chairs

& the open lid of his varnished casket
paper thin
gold taught on hallowed bone

more speckled somehow than when he prunes—
in the sun—
your family's mandarin tree

"the beginning of everything is the mother of everything"

—TAO TE CHING

IN THESE CONVERSATIONAL INTERJECTIONS THAT I AM ONCE MARRIED

he asks your name & repeats the sounds back
i don't tell him it means *great cloud*
but you are actually earth

how your parents see me for the river i am
& i erode your soil
i worry about the afterlife repercussions

of breaking a heart
i wonder about the day i am not there for
when you smile & realize we are better off

i am unsure what to do with trinkets i keep
bringing from abandoned rooms
i lose the key

to that jewelry box you help me haggle down in a beijing alley
the puzzle box where you hide my engagement ring
now has a stuck ball bearing

who do i give this furniture to when i pull off the dusty sheets?
sunray particles spell out that first weekend we meet—
three generations of your family drive towards canada in a van

pause in portland
so i can lay eyes on you & kiss someone
for the first time

i am in love with eight months of internet love
we go to the zoo in rain
my navy wool sweater itches

we spend sunday morning on a damp bench
in a concrete tunnel holding hands &
watching sturgeon swim

WHAT CRASHES INSIDE

the sea is calling me but i avoid it
trough after crest patiently rolls in while i pretend
i'm smaller than ocean

we go to disneyland instead
distract ourselves with pleasure on this sun wheel—
dangle above lights reflected in chlorinated

shallows nothing like ocean
i curl to fit
in your delicate family with my broad shoulders

your parents call me *white ghost girl*
i sleep in your bed
they warn again that *fire covers eyes*

i am unsure what it says about passion that in nine years
we never forget a condom—
not when we move four miles from waves in the tidy duplex

where every surface has too many layers of gloss paint
or later in the half-million-dollar post-war
tract home we go in debt for—

i never tell you about the afternoon
your grandmother doesn't recognize my ghost
leaving phö 79 three summers after

you & i quit softly over sushi
i tell my gran it's over & she says
well those orientals sure are different aren't they sis?

which is racist
i go back to ocean
run alone with it since i no longer break at your shore

feel it swell inside of me
opposite of how we never make a baby
i no longer pretend this body isn't almost all water

discover how little say i have about flow
yes i allow gran *they are different*
only i remember she & your grandmother trade

laughter instead of common tongue at our wedding
shoulder to shoulder
twenty old swollen knuckles

from long cleaner shifts starching uniforms during the war
from sewing bras for nickels in a sweatshop downtown
in the ocean foam

i remember how far from ocean i start from
coal hills of south dakota
where my gran is the small scared girl of a fire-tempered miner

who drives west with her big sister
in the ocean foam
i remember how far from ocean you start from

a dirt floor in a village at the base of a steppe farm
where months after her young husband dies
your grandmother births your father

WE EAT FAMILY-STYLE & OUR PROGENY ARE THEORETICAL

bite-sized barbecue waits under fly screens
the table is covered in felt-backed vinyl left from christmas
overlapped again with newsprint

chairs don't match & we near always sit in the same order
ma   ba   a-màh   a-yèh   big sister   little brother
                                                         me   you

once we marry your *ma* tries to feed me auspicious
fertility roots in the shape of infant penises
we don't want one you say & push away the bowl

besides i add after dinner & point to potential adoption
your father is peeling pummelo & erupts
in english your mother & grandparents cannot understand

blood matters
you can never love a baby as much that isn't your own
one seat away your *a-yèh* is not your *ba's* blood kin

i don't bring up i get my own daddy by being taken in
citrus rind is torn and tossed on sunday comics
i stay quiet

OUR MOTHERS ARE DIFFERENT

my mama makes scrambled eggs whipped with milk
or half-n-half if the fridge has some to offer
quite a bit of black pepper

cooked patiently with a whole lot of butter
so this how i make eggs but sometimes
i still make eggs like your *ma*

stirred hard into a quarter cup of oil
wok hot & black
poured thin & folded quickly with chopped scallion

your *ma* who tells you to tell me to get a sweater
your *ma* who tells you to tell me to drink ginseng soup
your *ma* who tells you that i should like pink

she wishes i was softer
but not like how my thighs are pillows
she requests an innocence undone

i am unaccustomed to
a mother who wants me to be a child
even in a small body i am my mama's confidante

my mama tells me i am her savior
my softness isn't in girlish hand holding
how small ones do

without even thinking of kissing
my softness is in the rupture of my aorta
at the dull thud of a fish counter club

in 99 ranch market with your *ma*
who asks me to pick one out
& while i know i'm ending it i don't expect

that pain to burst into my throat
striking me cold-blooded & rainbow-scaled
if only for a moment

for nine years i cannot speak
to her without your middle-man
translation but warm

to her cheekbone
supple with the three economical freckles
your *ma*'s soft

skin—rose pink
when she weeps like my mama
i collect our family trees' melancholies

braid them leaf by stem into an avalanche reminder i still sleep under
our mothers—
they cry tears for us

"what works reliably is to know the raw silk, hold the uncut wood"

—TAO TE CHING

"NOWHERE DO I WANT TO REMAIN FOLDED"

because where i am
bent and folded,
there i am lie

part tissue paper
part razor thin lead
part lace vein of a preserved oak leaf

i am accordioned diligently
a pleated fan to fit skin
bent in half & then again across the seams until

my folds are less basic geometry
& more the organic lines in the palms of hands
a paper may be folded seven times

but i am creased many more than that
this imprint mapped by unbundling
at points divine

lacking in visible sense sometimes
i want to unfold
sometimes unroll

sometimes quietly
sometimes not without tearing
i unfold

in time i cannot know
a barely formed beak suddenly believes
it is enough to pierce shell

THIS PENDULUM OF AWAY, ERASE, RETURN, FUSE, RECLEAVE

my new lover's hair is longer but his beard is gone
shaved clean every day he lives onboard
for fire respirators & happy corporate overlords

whiskers grow more slowly than how he & i fall
back comfortable after one night—
then two—still barely stubble

by next week the red parts translucent in light return
& also coin-sized patches of pure white
under his jaw he is too young for

when he travels to his parents' for the weekend
i am a thing i never think i'll be again—
some secret two plane rides away—

like that night i meet you across a chat screen
it's late & we sit on an imaginary roof peak
you toss my doc martens off to keep me longer

he & you are first-born american generations
your sacrificial parents suspicious of love
i think about how you have red in your beard too

i think about everything your father ever says
about me but never to me
& how many of those things i make true when i leave

i read you remarry an australian
i consider mailing you this leather satchel that is yours
but becomes mine for all of college & after

the handle needs repaired
i don't want the story around anymore
only i leave it at the goodwill

since it seems best not to reach out
after that email two years ago has no answer
after the awkward lunch four years before that

where your eyes can't make sense of my metamorphosis
& i cry
when you casually mention

(not expecting they keep it secret)
how my gran & gramp fall for a travel money scam
when the caller steals your identity

STRETCHING FARTHER BACK THAN MATH, EVER PRESENT WISDOM IF I LET IT

i grow my hair long & light again
after it gets short & black when i leave
because i learn if i am not blonde more people listen to what i say

barely back to my nipples like how
strands cover me when my breasts are sixteen
the second time we share space-time

you & i spend five sleepness nights in a hide-a-bed
i take my shirt off but keep my crushed blue velvet bottoms on
my w.w.j.d. wristband is on the nightstand

the year before ashley judd is my first girl crush
double jeopardy loops while i do calculus
you're on the line helping me calculate derivatives

i know only your typing syntax & voice
husky & licking some notion of me through a corded phone—
clear with neon internals—

i cry
convinced you will never want to touch me this way
in real life

there is this body but also some thought virus
that despises it & most other parts of most other bodies
on the sidewalk i judge ankles too fat

who gives me this story?
now thirty-three
body feeling worthless but how hard my spleen works

instead of going to two parties
i take off my clothes
never make it to the shower

text my new lover this picture—
shadow curve of pelvis
a triangle too many weeks from waxing—

when he stumbles on a *seventeen* article
teaching how to touch a vulva
he wonders to me why instructions are needed

then backtracks—*well women have explained to me*
it's hard to see what's going on down there without a mirror
he asks me to recount the first twinges

i tell him of fingertip whorls electrocuting bone
accidentally somehow certain
a finite amount of thrill exists

in an innocent span of belly skin
dark—only bright light in the distant door
a black towel on a golden rack & a mirror that never measures up

i am beating
i say to the pulsing
cosmos in stillness

nothing in this room moves
except for my blood
a swelling in my eardrums makes your voice far away

IN & OUT OF THE ACHE OF THIS TEN-TOED SHAPE

i won't tell my gran i sleep with doors locked
at this foreign rest stop
where i acupressure my glands (like i learn from you)

until discomfort drains
& i use the toilet in black night certain i will find
some wild mess of reflection

instead a creature in the mercury mirror—
irises clear
humid curls of champagne rain—

stuns me back to where i cannot drown
sounds with demands that never pause linear
a lack of slumber grows a canker

my canine catches every time i whisper
i am finally here
in a ford fiesta wearing damp socks hours before

i buy a black journal &
the first sight of the *grand palais* gives me shivers
i fantasize about finding myself

in a park after dawn where i will sit & listen
to joni sing *california, i'm coming home*
from this old cold city

my companion's rise & fall may be sleep or
only stillness
i am finally comfortable

in the dark searching for symbols i do not know yet
under water-pinged tin
wide-eyed at my more beautiful ghost who visits

"what's softest in the world rushes and runs over what's hardest in the world"

—TAO TE CHING

I REMEMBER HOW TO TRANSMUTE WHAT I CAN'T FORGET

i open a notebook i buy with you twelve years ago
in a hong kong super market
to find a recipe in my hand

i can't recall writing
chant thohh 6x
hold breath 6 seconds x 3

chant mayy 6x
imagine the third eye closed
imagine the third eye opening as if from sleep

this key opens a red door to a forest womb encircling
unending gold hair
language is no good here but sound is pleasure

my higher being nude
embodied but hardly solid
sitting legs crossed in root cradle

under an overturned clump of moss
pried up with bare fingers is a wood box
i offer myself this gift of the same scent

of the card catalogue at the public library when i am six
full of yellowing scraps typewritten & cross-referenced
every sliver of occasion since this body's inception

the first year i know you
you mail me three books in a box set
romance unfolds in handwritten post

between lovers trapped in different dimensions
my favorite illustration is the puffy cheeked goldfish
swimming through a shattered wine glass like a bullet

then i think how poetic
this tale of yearning
while you sleep one thousand & thirty six miles from me

ever in our own dimension
even when we overlap
by postman

or happenstance
i keep the art books
i burn your letters

A MAGE SHOWS ME THERE IS A WOMB BIG ENOUGH TO HOLD ALL OF ME

she & i sit on my floor lit by the glow
of prayer candles i use for light after sundown
even though i am not catholic

i confess a secret i never whisper to my mama
that i am happy my biological father doesn't come around
how i am shaped by never being owned by a man

the mage tells me this is also important to her
at my wedding i walked myself down the aisle
but when you & i marry my daddy does walk me

the man my mama & i make ours after i already speak
surely i am his daughter but *i am* before i am *his*
i always feel you sense

i am only my own
on our wedding day
in the grass before doves fly

my arm is in my daddy's & he & i cry
at some unnamable ending
that picture is still on my gran's mantel—

one raw moment that outlives any promise i make to you
i return to the mage in this flickering room who says
when i first encountered you i wasn't ready for what you are

may I hold your hand?
i grow until the mirror marking some edge of my sense
                                              reaches another sun star
we are not ready for what we are

AFTERWARD

i forgive you
for everything you did not & could not know

i forgive me
for everything i did not & could not know

RELEASE AT THE PROMPT OF AN ELEGY

this deceiving current with an undertow toward ocean
& surface wind-plied opposite
is the stick still or moving?

how long do i want to stand on a draw bridge to decide?
my cheeks are stinging cold
my low back is sweating

i am somewhere in both & neither
hearing syllables i reel in since summer
old stories i don't see coming

clear like fish line clothes-lining me
i cast inside for whatever else will snag
like an article i see

how to really cleanse past lovers' energy & it works
but i only read the headline
never click the link

any last piece of driftwood
trash
a shiny crow bauble

until the net once brimming & left to sort later
is turned out & air dried

be well my love

NOTES

The four quoted lines that serve as section markers in this chapbook ("the thirteen organs of our living are the thirteen organs of our dying;" "the beginning of everything is the mother of everything;" "what works reliably is to know the raw silk, hold the uncut wood;" and "what's softest in the world rushes and runs over what's hardest in the world") are taken from *Lao Tzu's Tao Te Ching: A New English Version* by Ursula K. Le Guin (Shambhala, 1997).

On page 34, the quoted title and first stanza, "Nowhere do I want to remain folded, because where I am bent and folded, there I am lie" as well as the line "I want to unfold" are taken from Rainer Maria Rilke's poem "I am too alone in the world" found in *Rilke's Book of Hours: Love Poems to God* (Penguin, 2005).

ACKNOWLEDGMENTS

With awe & reverence to my fellow poet & mage K. M. Lighthouse for her striking inspiration & magic.

Gratitude to Dawn Thompson, Birch Dwyer, Beth Melnick and my other sisters in Portland Women Writers for holding space in writing circles where it is a great joy to cultivate my voice, witness others & be seen. To Lauren Paredes, Andrew Chenevert, Caroline Wilcox Reul & the many poets in Portland's Eastside Poetry Workshop for their time spent reflecting on these poems and earlier versions of this manuscript.

Peace to *you*—may these sounds breathe some kind of freedom for both our young selves.

ASH GOOD was born in Paradise, California, and raised in a small Oregon mill town. She is the author of *sounds in my möbius mind* (First Matter Press) and *These things will never happen quite like that again* (LettersAt3AMPress). Ash is the founder of High Priestesses of Poetry & holds sacred space for story tellers to connect with their highest self & healer within. She lives in Portland, Oregon.

www.ingramcontent.com/pod-product-compliance
Lightning Source LLC
Chambersburg PA
CBHW051603010526
44118CB00023B/2807